RHEUM

Outlines the va... arthritis, their common causes and safe corrective measures, which include vitamin therapy, hydrotherapy and the ideal diet for sufferers of these distressing ailments.

RHEUMATISM
AND ARTHRITIS

•

An outline of common causes
and safe corrective measures

•

*Prepared and produced by the Editorial Committee
of Science of Life Books*

•

SCIENCE OF LIFE BOOKS
4-12 Tattersalls Lane, Melbourne, Victoria 3000

Thirteenth Edition 1969
Fourth Impression 1973
Fourteenth Edition (revised and reset) 1975
Second Impression 1976
Third Impression 1977
Fourth Impression 1978

Registered at the G.P.O. Sydney,
for transmission through the post
as a book.

National Library of Australia card number
and ISBN 0 909911 64 9 (paperback)
ISBN 0 909911 90 8 (hardback)

Typeset by Specialised Offset Services, Liverpool
and printed by Weatherby Woolnough, Wellingborough
Northants, England

CONTENTS

INTRODUCTION

Rheumatism in its various forms is one of the most common ailments to which human flesh is heir, and none produces so much pain or creates so many cripples, either partly or wholly, as does rheumatism. No human ailment interferes so much with a man's or a woman's work, and yet, incongruous as it may seem, no ailment is easier to understand in its causation and remedy than rheumatism.

The roots of rheumatism lie in a faulty diet and in habitual overeating of unsuitable and acid-forming foods, especially those that are deficient in the essential vitamins. Those vitamins most relevant to the prevention and relief of rheumatism are the B complex and vitamin C, although vitamin A, D and E are also important. In fact rheumatic and arthritic patients often have a history of respiratory tract infections such as colds, bronchitis and laryngitis, which indicates a lack of vitamins A and C in the system.

Similarly, many people with rheumatism or arthritis have digestive troubles, or suffer from excessive fatigue and are underweight, which suggests a shortage of the B complex vitamins in their diet. And laboratory tests made on animals by placing them on diets low in vitamin C have resulted in conditions that closely resemble human arthritis. All of which serves to emphasize that rheumatic ailments are not inevitable, but rather that they are the legacy of many years of indiscriminate feeding.

This book sets out to provide the sufferer with the necessary knowledge and inspiration to change his or her ways to those which will lead towards the restoration of health.

MAIN RHEUMATIC CATEGORIES

Muscular Rheumatism: This term explains itself. It is rheumatism of the muscles, usually referred to as fibrositis. Generally only one group of muscles is affected at a time, such as muscles of the shoulder, neck, back, loins, arms or leg.

The symptoms need not indicate a serious condition. It is often caused by draught or a chill. The cold draught or chill constricts the blood vessels in the affected region. Thus the toxic matter in that region is not eliminated, and inflammation is set up. This localized condition calls for simple, local treatment, and usually passes after copious sweating has been induced, as mentioned later in this book.

Fibrositis is also caused by injury to a part – a muscle, tendon, or ligament. Here again, the localized treatment is generally effective. When fibrositis is the result of a chill or injury, one should take a vitamin C (250 mg) tablet three times daily after meals, and a vitamin A capsule (2,500 units), once a day only.

Where muscular rheumatism or fibrositis shows signs of becoming chronic and cannot be explained by draughts, chills or injury, then one must look for the cause in the excess acidity in the average diet. Indeed there is little doubt that most cases of rheumatism in its several forms, whether fibrositis, lumbago, arthritis or osteo-arthritis, etc., are caused by excess acidity in the diet, but we will deal with that later.

Rheumatoid Arthritis

Rheumatoid Arthritis is primarily a disease of the covering about the joint. It is described as 'a disease of the joints characterized by morbid changes in the synovial membrane surrounding the smaller joints, cartilage and bones. It results in deformity, restricted movement of joints affected, and muscular wasting."

The disease is familiar to most of us, for we have seen all too frequently those joint changes involving the terminal and other finger joints. Sometimes they have become greatly enlarged. Some of the nodes (knobs or hard tumors) give little trouble except mentally, but that is trouble enough when one is aware of the possible progress of the disease.

Sometimes there is distortion of hands and wrists also, for although it particularly affects the smaller joints, the larger ones, including the elbows, frequently become affected. The joints are usually affected in the following order: Hands, feet, wrists, ankles, knees and cervical vertebrae; but no joint is immune.

At first the inflammation attacks only the fibrous tissues around the joint, but unless the disease is arrested, the synovial membranes and articular cartilages will also become chronically inflamed. The cartilages may ultimately show excessive destruction, with the heads of the bones becoming bare. In some cases the movement of the joints causes a creaking and grating sound.

Women sufferers are the more numerous; some give the ratio as three to one, some as high as five to one and the onset, in most cases, occurs before forty years of age. If nothing is done to remove the causes, the joints gradually lose their flexibility, becoming enlarged, distorted, and finally immovable. In other words, the bone becomes fixed to the socket by a slow, but insidious process of mineralization.

The excess acidity in the blood stream saturates not only muscles (causing fibrositis) but is deposited in the form of urates, or uric acid salts in the joints. They become inflamed, painful and enlarged and gradually movement becomes difficult; finally impossible. These adhesions are referred to as 'ankylosis', i.e., fixation of a joint.

Osteo-arthritis

Osteo-arthritis usually makes its onset later in life than does rheumatoid, and its manifestation is more gradual. Unlike rheumatoid arthritis, it is less frequent in women than in men.

Unlike the sufferer from rheumatoid arthritis, who is usually underweight, though not always, those afflicted by osteo-arthritis are mostly robust people, who have led a healthy out-of-doors existence. They may never have had anything the matter with them till their joints became troublesome.

In osteo-arthritis it is less the surrounding tissues of

the joints that are affected than the bones and the cartilage on which they move. Degeneration sets in, but there is also an increase in some of the cells so that the shape of the head of the bone may change.

Over-use of a joint is a partial explanation but in many instances, there is undoubtedly a disturbance of the body's chemistry. A toxic bowel may explain at least some of the arthritis, and in women the cessation of the menstrual flow contributes to the changes which take place in the knees and fingers.

One feature that is characteristic of the osteo-arthritic form is that the disease is not likely to spread to the other joints as in rheumatoid arthritis; but the handicap can be severe enough even when only one joint is afflicted.

Osteo-arthritis results in a mineralized-deposit enlargement of the larger joints (those of the neck, hips, knees, back, or fingers). Most patients are over 40 and are often overweight.

Lumbago, Neuritis, Sciatica

Lumbago is a rheumatic condition affecting the muscles of the lower part of the back – that part known as the lumbar region. Unless cured by the proper principles, it gets more frequent and more painful – like all rheumatic complaints – as the sufferer gets older.

Neuritis is rheumatism or inflammation of the sciatic nerve, which runs down each hip joint. It is a particularly crippling complaint and agonizing in its painfulness. The sciatic nerve is the longest nerve in the body and runs clear down to the ankle. Lumbago and sciatica can be caused by draught, dampness or chill, and, therefore, properly treated, need not become chronic. They can also arise from a displaced spinal disc or vertebra, and the services of a competent osteopath or chiropractor should be sought if the diet and vitamins suggested fail to bring relief.

Gout

We quote from *Diseases of Joints and Rheumatic Affections*:

'Gout is popularly supposed to be a rich man's disease, but it is just as much in evidence among the poor.

'It is essentially a disease of wrong living – whether of "high living" or "low living" does not really matter.

'In addition to faulty diet, the gouty individual stands convinced of a tendency to drink too much intoxicating liquor, to take too little exercise, and generally to undermine his constitution in various ways.

'The disease consists in a great excess of urates and uric acid in the blood and tissues, and shows marked preference for the joints of the feet in particular. In many cases chalky deposits (lime salts) appear in the joints.

'In an attack of gout, the big toe joints are first affected.'

An important therapeutic factor in curing gout is vitamin B_1. But other vitamins are also important, and the vitamin therapy, dosage and diet given later in this book, should be followed (see page 60).

Poultices of comfrey give great relief in gout. Comfrey tablets are available and can be crushed and mixed with olive oil, then spread on lint and applied externally.

Spondylitis

Spondylitis is a chronic, progressive disease of arthritic origin which affects one or more of the vertebrae. The degenerative changes in the vertebrae are similar to those seen in rheumatoid arthritis. Ninety per cent of patients with spondylitis are males, often young men. The onset is usually gradual, beginning with mild back pains which become increasingly severe as the inflammation intensifies.

Bursitis

Bursitis means inflammation of a bursa or bursae. A bursa is a small flattened sac, namely, a pouch, containing synovial fluid, a slippery lubricant required to reduce friction and absorb shocks at joints and tendons. These bursae are interposed between parts of the body that move on each other. The bursae most commonly the cause of trouble are those at the elbow ('tennis elbow') the shoulder joint, and the knee joint ('housemaid's knee').

The most frequent cause of bursitis is an injury, such as a knock or unusual pressure on the kneecap, or an excessive amount of exercise which can irritate the shoulder joint and elbow bursae (tennis elbow).

Heavy lifting such as women engage in when bringing home goods after shopping, can cause bursitis in shoulders and elbows. The turning of wringers attached to some older model washing machines, can also lead to bursitis. Other and more rare forms of bursitis are caused by acute or chronic infection and need not concern us here. Contributing factors are an unsatisfactory diet containing inadequate protein, also overwork, and lack of sleep.

Hot fomentations should be applied and the affected part rested and gently massaged. Later, gentle passive movement of the joint may be made and increased gradualiy until normal action of the joint is restored.

The following should be taken three times daily, after meals (all together), namely:

4 Vitamin B_{12} tablets	0.025 mg
3 Rutin tablets	60 mg
1 Vitamin E tablet	50 mg
1 Lecithin capsule	250 mg
3 Calcium tablets (white)	60 mg

and

1 dessertspoonful brewers' yeast powder, mixed in milk or water.

Rheumatic Fever

It is now recognized that rheumatic fever is associated with a prior streptococcal (bacterial) infection. Overcrowding, malnutrition and dampness all predispose to respiratory infections and thereby indirectly to rheumatic fever.

This fever often develops into rheumatic heart disease, namely, a crippling of the heart's valvular action, thereby interfering with the passage of blood to and from the heart with a consequent disturbance of bodily function.

Rheumatic fever usually begins with a sore throat,

tonsillitis, or scarlet fever. Cough, chill, fever, pleurisy and abdominal pains may be experienced. Joint pains of a severe nature generally follow and continue for some days.

According to *The Lancet*, investigations made in New York revealed that in a school for girls of wealthy parents, there had not been a case of rheumatic fever for ten years, whereas among poor children living near the school, there were many cases. *The British Medical Journal* found that there was a reduction in the number of cases of rheumatic fever when children ate eggs as part of their diet. Research indicated that patients had been eating too little protein food.

It would seem therefore that sound nutrition and healthy housing will effectively prevent most cases of rheumatic fever. Vitamin E has been found beneficial in restoring to health those whose hearts have been damaged by rheumatic heart disease, following their having contracted rheumatic fever, usually in their early youth. The vitamin E dosage in an initial attack, calls for 400 mg daily, irrespective of age.

In subsequent attacks where there may be extensive injury to the heart, it is prudent to begin with 100 mg of vitamin E daily for two weeks and increase the daily dosage slowly by 20 mg every month, until four to five hundred mg are being taken daily.

CAUSES OF
RHEUMATIC AILMENTS

In orthodox medical circles rheumatism in its various forms is usually attributed to infected teeth or tonsils or to the weather. To say that rheumatism is due to abscessed teeth or infected tonsils is only partly true. The teeth and tonsils in themselves were probably poisoned in the first place by a toxic blood stream. To extract the teeth or cut out the tonsils merely deals with the effect. It does not remove the cause of the toxic body condition. This is invariably proved by the fact that rheumatic sufferers only get temporary relief by the removal of teeth and tonsils. The rheumatism invariably returns unless the basic cause of the toxic condition is cleared up.

'Suspicious teeth', according to one eminent authority, 'rarely cause a true arthritis, and there has often been the needless sacrifice of these and of various organs of the body.' In an article on 'Arthritis Therapy', Charles Rudolph, M.D., of New York, said: 'The vogue of removing foci of infection, real or imaginary, has, unfortunately, largely overshadowed all other methods of treatment.'

One US authority (Carl Richard Wise, M.D.) says: 'It is generally accepted that removal of foci of

infection does no good and the useless removal of
tonsils and teeth is to be avoided.'

Weather

As for the weather causing rheumatism – this has no
basis of fact. If this is true, then the people of the cold,
wet countries, such as the British Isles, Northern
Europe and Russia would be martyrs to rheumatism.

The fact is that the people of these countries do not
suffer any more from this ailment that the people of
Australia. Indeed, some authorities say that the
incidence of rheumatism is more general in Australia
than in the European countries named. Undoubtedly
the rheumatic sufferer reacts to sudden changes in the
weather, but this is because his condition is affected by
the weather. This is very different from saying that his
rheumatism was caused by the weather.

Damp, chilly weather does, however, depress the
circulation and cold draughts can lower one's
resistance by causing constriction of the blood vessels.
This interferes with the elimination of waste products
from the muscles and surrounding areas, thereby
setting up an inflammatory condition conducive to
fibrosis. To take drugs is futile because local
treatment, i.e., steam baths, or hot and cold
compresses are needed, as discussed elsewhere in this
book.

It should be borne in mind that a faulty diet will
load the body with toxic substances, so that an attack
of fibrositis will be more severe, and of longer duration
than if the body's powers of resistance were higher.

The ills of winter are partly due to the fact that we are denied the benefit of summer's perspiration, and thus accumulate additional poisons in the system which lower our resistance to epidemics. In addition, in winter we eat more freely of the heating, acid-forming foods, and eat less of the vitalizing fruits and salad vegetables.

Rheumatism is often the result of an accumulation of acidity in the muscles or joints. By building up the alkalinity of the blood stream and by adequate and regular elimination, without the assistance of purgative medicines, the severity of attacks may be lessened and in many cases averted.

The Acid-forming Foods

The basic cause of most forms of rheumatism is an acid blood stream, due to a diet consisting largely of acid-forming foods.

The acid-forming foods are:

Meat	Alcholic liquors
Fish	Macaroni and Spaghetti
Poultry	Sugar
Oysters	Jam
Cheese	Fried foods
Eggs	Strong tea
Bread	Coffee
Flour	Common salt
Pastry	Sauces
Pies	Condiments
Rice	Pickles
Confectionery	Condensed milk

'Soft' Drinks
Cakes
Biscuits

Pre-cooked and
processed cereals

Acidity: Parent of Disease

If you who suffer from rheumatism will check over
the foregoing list of foods, you will see that these are
the foods which have made up the bulk of your diet all
the days of your life. They are acid-forming and
acidity is often the parent of rheumatism.

You may reply that the foods listed constitute the
diet of 95 per cent of the people of this country, and
that many people seem to be able to eat this acid-
forming food year after year without getting
rheumatism. Yet nobody knows exactly how far these
apparently immune people have progressed,
unbeknown to themselves, towards a rheumatic
condition.

It doesn't follow, of course, that everybody who eats
the acid-forming foods we have listed will contract
rheumatism. But one thing is certain: practically every
human being who persists with an acid-forming diet,
unleavened with a preponderance of alkaline-forming
fruits and vegetables, will very likely eventually fall
victim to rheumatism, kidney disease, heart disease,
high blood-pressure, or chronic ill-health.

Like chrity, nature suffereth long. But there is a
limit to her tolerance, and finally she calls a halt.

Ten Causes of Rheumatism

The usual causes of rheumatism in its various forms are as follows:

1. Excessive eating. The British, European and American feeding tradition is one of excess food consumption.

The average man or woman does not need more than one-third to one-half of the food usually eaten. A breakfast of cereal and milk, followed by eggs or grilled and fried vegetables, toast, tea or coffee, is beyond the digestive capacity of everybody except those people doing hard physical work. The average lunch is also excessive; while an evening meal of meat, vegetables and sweets merely adds insult to injury. This excessive food intake creates more uric acid than can be eliminated by the kidneys and sweat glands.

2. Too much meat and starchy food. The protein foods (meat, fish, eggs or cheese) leave no waste bulk to stimulate the bowel action. Instead, they leave an acid ash, which has chiefly to be eliminated through the kidneys. The kidneys are not equal to the task, and the uric acid accumulates in the blood stream, causing rheumatism.

The offending starchy foods are usually white bread, processed breakfast foods, stodgy porridges, polished rice, pappy biscuits and pastry – all of which are largely devitalized and demineralized. They are not desirable foods – merely causes of fermentation, congestion, constipation, acidity and rheumatism.

3. Incompatible food combinations. The fermentation of which we speak is especially acute when we eat incompatible foods at the same meal,

such as protein foods and concentrated starch foods, or acid fruits, stewed or raw, with white bread or pastry.

Why Digestion Breaks Down

4. *Indiscriminate feeding.* Most of us have grown up in the evil dietetic tradition that all so-called food is good for one – that it's all 'grist for the mill'.

We therefore proceed to eat anything and everything that comes our way, quite regardless of the appalling task we have set out digestive organs, our eliminatory organs and the chemistry of the body itself. Soup, meat, vegetables, messy puddings, washed down by tea or coffee – down it all goes. We may arise from such a meal with a strong sense of satisfaction, but we have set in motion all the factors which may finally create fermentation, flatulence, acidity and – rheumatism.

5. If that were not bad enough, our next meal may add to the offence by consisting of one or other of the doubtful concoctions, pleasing enough to look at, no doubt, which fill the windows of the delicatessen shop.

Here we see a picturesque assortment of embalmed, preserved and demineralized products masquerading as 'food' in the form of pies, pastries, pickled pork, pickled onions, corned beef, pig's trotters, and an assortment of sausage meats, consisting of meat scraps, flour, fat and colouring, highly flavoured and seasoned – all acid-forming, all aiders and abettors of rheumatism in one or other of its forms.

Condiments and Sugar

6. Condiments are a further potent contribution to an acid blood stream.

7. Sugar also stands indicted for its acid-forming qualities. To quote from *Your Diet in Health and Disease* by Harry Benjamin:

'All refined sugar is useless, needless, and harmful, as it requires a great deal of oxygen for its combustion in the tissues and prevents the oxygen being used for other and more important purposes.

'In addition, the heat it generates, not being required for the work of the body generally, is so much waste fuel, and the end products of its combustion being excessively acid, they require a proportionately large amount of mineral salts, which the body can ill afford, for their neutralization. . . .

8. The eating of devitalized, and demineralized foods, such as white bread, refined breakfast foods, biscuits, polished rice, etc. These are all acid-forming – all stepping stones to rheumatic ailments.

9. Excessive tea and coffee drinking. Both are acid-forming. Incidentally, wine is notorious for its formation of acidity.

10. A diet woefully deficient in vitamins A, the B complex vitamins, Vitamin C, D and E. The B complex vitamins and C are particularly important for the prevention – and the relief – of rheumatism.

The One Great Error

Broadly, the foregoing are the ten sins of commission

which, between them, give rise to an acid blood stream and finally rheumatism in one of its forms.

These sins of commission are aggravated by those who eat inadequately of the foods that alkalize the blood and give it its proper chemical balance. Such foods are the fresh fruits and salad vegetables, and to a lesser extent the dried and stewed fruits and the cooked vegetables.

Sir W. Arbuthnot Lane, one of Britain's greatest surgeons and nutritional authorities, wrote:

'There is no longer any doubt that all forms of rheumatism are due to disturbance of the acid-alkaline balance, and that this condition arises from faults in nutrition. Clinical experience has now amply proved that the physical factors which predispose some people to rheumatism can only be successfully countered by a diet which puts all its emphasis upon alkaline-forming foods.'

Dr Adrian Vander, a European authority upon modern medical science, has written in his book, *Rheumatism and Gout*:

'The whole group of rheumatic illnesses is nothing but the result of an abnormal, i.e., diseased, alteration in the composition of the bodily fluids.

'This has its origin in the first place in the acidification of the body (especially with uric acid and oxalic acid).

Four Sources of Acidity

Dr Howard Hay has stated that the four known sources of acid-formation in the body, according to modern medical science, are as follows:

(a) The use of too much of the concentrated foods: meats, eggs, fish, cheese, dried peas, beans, lentils, nuts, bread and all grain foods.

(b) The free use of those foods from which the normal alkalines are lost, as processed starches, sugar and sweets of all kinds, white bread, pastries, refined breakfast cereals; sugars, synthetic syrups, candies.

(c) The incompatible mixing of foods of all kinds, as the starches or surgars with either the acid fruits or the protein foods.

(d) The retention of food residues in the large bowel beyond the twenty-four hours that mark the outside limit of safety.

The Value of Acid Fruits

Dr N.W. Walker, a doctor of science, points out that lemon juice and grapefruit juice aid in the removal or dissolving of minerals which have formed deposits in the cartilage of the joints, as in arthritis, as the result of excessive consumption of acid-forming foods.

As a general rule, acid fruits are not acid forming; they neutralize body acids. But such fruits may aggravate the condition of sufferers from acute arthritis and rheumatism, as these people's digestive processes may not be able to deal with the juices and render them alkaline.

Other useful alkalizers for correcting excess acidity are alfalfa and such vegetables as celery, watercress parsley, mint and horse-radish. Alfalfa tablets, also vegetable tablets (containing the five above-mentioned vegetables, together with birch) all valuable for excess acidity, are available.

Rheumatism Can Be Arrested

Dr Howard Hay, when asked 'What is rheumatism? How can it be corrected?' supplied the following answer:

'Rheumatism is a general name for all sorts of painful inflammation about the joints and muscles, some of which are called arthritis, some simple rheumatism, acute, sub-acute, and chronic, some synovitis or water in the joint, and no doubt much neuritis passes as rheumatism.

'All these things are merely deposits of salts representing waste matter, or toxic-serum or lymph in the case of the watery infiltrations. These are to be corrected by neutralising the acidity and eliminating the waste, though it may be a slow process.

'In the case of arthritis, there are salts such as urates that are actually outside the circulation, deposited in the free joint cavity and not absorbable, usually so constituting a permanent crippling to just this extent.

'All forms are easily arrested, and all but arthritis recover easily and quickly under drastic detoxication and corrected diet.'

EFFECTS OF ORTHODOX THERAPIES

The orthodox approach to the problem of rheumatism in its several forms consists of medicines, pain-killing drugs, vaccines and gold injections, with embrocations, liniments and creams to rub in.

Clement Jeffrey, in his book, *Rheumatism*, wrote:

'While writing this book I have eagerly examined the best authorities for any guidance which I could give to the reader in the use of medicines for rheumatism; but drugs are a failure.

'I have mentioned that aspirin can give relief from pain, but it has the disadvantage of disturbing the digestion and producing an unnatural sweat.

'There can be little doubt that this perspiration is an attempt on the part of Nature to expel the aspirin from the system.

Dr Buckley states in his book on arthritis, fibrositis and gout that the number of drugs which have been tried in rheumatic diseases is legion. This, he adds, is a testimony to their general futility.

Dr Copeman in his book is even more outspoken. 'Drugs', he states, 'are comparatively useless in this disease except with the object of dulling pain and producing sleep.'

Gold Injections and Vaccines

What of gold salts? It is a serious thing, in our opinion, that gold, which does not belong to the constitution of the body, should be injected into the tissues. Even those who advocate this treatment emphasize the need for caution, and in some cases it is immediately dangerous. Gold is a cumulative drug. There is thus a risk of over-dosage if the injections are continued for some time.

Clement Jeffrey has written on this subject: 'I have had patients who had been given gold to cure their arthritis, but the only obvious results were ulcers of the mouth, a foetid breath, copious salivation and fever. These are all examples of Nature's efforts to eliminate the gold.'

This metal, or gold salt, is fraught with danger to vital tissues, and the *Journal of the American Medical Association* reported a case of fatal aplastic anaemia, following the use of gold-salt therapy. These injections are also liable to produce skin complaints, disturbances of the bowel, inflammation of the kidneys and neuralgia.

What of vaccines? These had a vogue some years ago for the treatment of rheumatoid arthritis, but their popularity waned as they failed to fulfil the hopes held out for them. Dr F.A. Robinson, in his book, *Attacking and Arresting Arthritis*, states: 'While vaccine is still being administered, many of the best authorities consider the treatment quite useless.'

Aspirins and A.P.C. Powders

Aspirins and A.P.C. powders are extensively advertised and are frequently stated as being 'good' for rheumatism. *The exact opposite is the truth*. They are pain-deadeners and do nothing to remove the *cause* of rheumatism. What is worse, they may poison the body and destroy the vitamins in the system, so that 'the last state is worse than the first.'

Testimonials for these drugs almost invariably conclude with 'I always carry a packet in my handbag' or 'We are never without them in the home', which is surely evidence that they do not cure but merely deaden the pain.

The price of the brief relief they give is to make the condition chronic.

Cortisone and ACTH

Cortisone and ACTH were originally hailed as 'wonder drugs' for the treatment of rheumatoid arthritis. So many 'wonder drugs' are dramatically announced, only to result in their great promise being tragically disappointing, that any new 'wonder drug' must be regarded with reservation until the claims made for it are definitely proved by extensive clinical experience.

Just what is ACTH? Where does it come from? How is it prepared? How does it act?

The letters ACTH stand for 'adrenocorticotrophic hormone'. This hormone, formed in the anterior lobe of the pea-sized pituitary gland at the base of the brain, is believed to stimulate the production of cortisone in the adrenal glands, one of which is located above each kidney. From this it would seem that ACTH, when injected, would stimulate the patient's own adrenal gland, thus making unnecessary the injection of cortisone.

For the preparation of ACTH, pituitary glands from slaughtered animals are used, preferably pigs' glands, which have been found to yield the highest percentage of ACTH per weight of gland. Sheep and oxen glands, in that order, are also used.

The glands, taken from the skulls as soon after death as possible, are put into acetone to preserve them. (It takes 1,500-1,800 pig pituitary glands to make up 1 lb. weight). Later, in the laboratory, the glands are minced, and the minced matter extracted and purified to give a crude ACTH fraction. This, further purified to a whitish powder, is only a minute percentage of the original gland matter, indicating that there is a very definite limit to the amount of ACTH which can be made available.

Disturbing Side Effects

As soon as cortisone came under public notice, mainly as a healing agent for arthritis sufferers, thousands were given new hope, if only because of the claims made for the drug overseas.

The same sort of thing happened with ACTH. But the important point to remember is that neither ACTH nor cortisone is a cure. They do not kill germs, nor do they remove toxins. They merely act as a shield between whatever is causing the illness, and the patient, PROVIDED THE ADMINISTRATION OF THE DRUG IS KEPT UP.

ACTH has been shown to act most effectively – but, unfortunately, most transiently – on sufferers from rheumatoid arthritis. They lose their pain, swelling and depression – UNTIL THE RELAPSE THAT COMES SO OFTEN AND SO SWIFTLY AFTER A MATTER OF HOURS.

The Mayo Clinic cites the case of a woman – a hopeless poly-arthritis cripple with no movement at all, who was transformed into a comfortable, happy person without pain – at the time of discharge from hospital. Two weeks later she returned in a wheel chair, her depression and poly-arthritic condition much worse than before.

But graver 'side effects' are being realized. For instance, Dr Gregory Schwartzman, of the Mt Sinai Hospital, New York, has shown that susceptibility to poliomyelitis is enhanced by the use of ACTH and cortisones. Other doctors believe that, administered unwisely, the hormone drugs may act detrimentally on the mentality of patients.

Lord Horder, physician to the late King George VI, in London issued this warning: 'Cortisone is giving us and will give us more rheumatic patients left at the stage where their disabilities require treatment, than before they had cortisone.'

Disillusionment

A leading Sydney Medical Practitioner writing in the

Sydney Sunday Telegraph said:

'As the months slip by, patients and doctors are being rapidly disillusioned about the new 'wonder drugs', ACTH and cortisone.

'These remedies have received great publicity, and as a result of this, many sick people are rushed into hospital for a great variety of conditions and diseases in order that these new drugs may be given a trial.

'The relatives are also anxious that everything that can be done should be done.

'The type and pattern of the response of the human body to these substances is now becoming fairly clear.

'Doctors are beginning to realise that they now *suppress* symptoms of various diseases, but do not have the slightest effect on the underlying cause.

'If the trouble is not serious, and is of short duration, cortisone makes the symptoms disappear until the disease runs its course.

'When treatment is stopped the patient feels and remains well.

'But if, on the other hand, the cause of the disease persists and the treatment is stopped symptoms return overnight, frequently with greater severity than before the treatment began.

'It does not do to take the use of these drugs too lightly.

'Sometimes death occurs while they are still under the influence of them, and gross psychological disturbances have been reported.

'This is a serious complication of their use . . .

'The present position is that the wonder has gone out of the 'wonder drugs', and we are left with a potent, but tricky remedy with which to fight symptoms, but not to cure disease.

Injurious Effects of Cortisone

In an article in the *Journal of the American Medical Association*, Paul H. Curtiss, Jr, M.D., Wm S. Clark, M.D., and Charles H. Herndon, M.D., describe four male patients with rheumatoid arthritis 'in whom severe compression fractures of the vertebrae have developed during the administration of cortisone or conticotropin or both.'

The authors go on to say, 'Although demineralization of the skeleton is a recognised complication of cortisone therapy, these cases have prompted the authors to emphasize the importance of possible pathological fractures when prolonged treatment of this nature is used.'

In other words, it is quite well known among physicians that giving cortisone may result in drawing the minerals out of the bones of patients so that the bones fracture or break.

In one of the cases described, a fifty-seven-year-old man was given cortisone and corticotropin for arthritis. After six months on cortisone, the doctors stopped giving it and the patient's temperature shot up. So they gave him corticotropin. When he came back to the hospital about two years later (we assume he had been taking the drugs all this time) he had the 'moon-face' and the 'buffalo hump' that seem to accompany long dosage with cortisone, also a haemorrhaging disorder of his skin. An x-ray showed that there was 'partial collapse' of five vertebrae.

A sixty-seven-year-old patient who had also been taking cortisone for arthritis had a fracture of one vertebrae and 'extensive generalized demineralization' of all the vertebrae. The third patient was a nine-year-old boy suffering from arthritis. In this case, too, there were fractures and 'demineralization' of the vertebrae. The fourth case was that of a sixty-five-year-old man whose x-rays showed fractures of two vertebrae and two ribs, and osteoporosis (a softening of the bone) in his thigh bones. The authors explain that such conditions are apparently the result of excessive loss of calcium, phosphorus and nitrogen, presumably caused by the cortisone.

Medical Journals' Warning

Articles from the *Journal of the American Medical Association*, the *Cambria County Medical Society Bulletin*, the *British Medical Journal*, *The Lancet*, and the *International Medical Digest*, pointed out that:

1. Cortisone paralyzes the body's natural defences against infection.

2. Cortisone may produce harmful symptoms in tuberculosis, schizophrenia, diabetes and peptic ulcer.

3. Cortisone masks the symptoms by which doctors recognize the progress of diseases in patients, so that the disease may go right on its deadly way while the patient feels good enough to go back to work. If the cortisone is withdrawn, symptoms will probably return and may be even worse. Or the patient may contract some infectious disease since his defences against infection have been lowered.

An article by Dr Walter C. Alvarez in his column *Your Health*, indicates that autopsies of many patients who had taken cortisone (for only five days in some cases) showed atrophy of the adrenal glands. What do you suppose has become of these glands by the time the patient has taken cortisone over a period of several years? There seems to be little chance that they could be coaxed back to normal functioning again. In addition, administration of cortisone may bring about severe reactions on such varied parts as the skin, kidneys, blood, sex organs, hair, stomach, mind and personality, nerves, heart and blood vessels.

Phenylbutazone

A drug currently being widely prescribed for arthritis is phenylbutazone. It is sold under various trade names and two physicians at the Royal Perth Hospital, W.A., have given details of patients elsewhere who developed leukaemia after being treated with phenylbutazone. Some of these patients subsequently died from leukaemia. Indeed, the makers of one brand of this drug admit that cases of leukaemia have been reported after its use, and advise doctors that all patients receiving it should have periodic blood counts.

NATURAL REMEDIAL PRINCIPLES

In the meantime, many people in all parts of the world have proved that the following principles, consistently and resolutely followed month after month, will in time improve the condition of rheumatoid arthritis or osteo-arthritis.

In the case of elderly people, with a long standing condition of rheumatoid-arthritis, the curative principles cannot be expected to remedy, but they will greatly relieve the condition and vastly improve the general health.

The same principles will correct the simpler forms of rheumatism such as fibrositis, in a matter of months.

Here are the curative principles:

The first step to the cure of this universal complaint is to STOP CAUSING IT. By that we mean the dead, devitalized acid-forming foods, listed earlier in this book, must form no part of your daily diet.

If your rheumatic condition is bad, cut down on meat for a while. If it is not so bad take a little meat with compatible food combinations. Cut down your bread to two slices of wholemeal bread daily. Dispense with porridge and breakfast cereals altogether.

Substitute wheat-germ, milk and fruit.

Diluted fruit juices rich in vitamin C should be taken daily – orange, lemon, grapefruit, pineapple or apple juice. Get rid of the fallacy that acid fruits create acidity. They do just the opposite. Their reaction in the blood is 100 per cent alkaline. All acid fruits are wonderful in alkalizing the blood, except — as already stated – in cases of acute arthritis and rheumatism.

Remember, the benefit obtained depends on just one factor: how well you succeed in changing an acid, poisoned. unhealthy blood stream into a blood stream with the proper acid-alkaline balance, free from poisonous debris, and carrying a normal blood supply to every organ, every muscle, every nerve in your body.

If you succeed, your rheumatism will rapidly or gradually disappear, depending upon your condition when you began the treatment.

Not only that, but poor health will give way to better health, and misery to happiness. Your cure and your happiness are in your own hands.

In all your eating adopt this essential principle. See that your daily diet consists of about three-quarters of alkaline-forming foods, and only about one quarter of the acid-forming foods, and make sure that your diet is supplemented with the vitamins mentioned later in this book under 'Vitamin Dosage'.

Raw Food for Rheumatics

Tests carried out by British medical men on people suffering with all types of rheumatic ailments and reported in the *Proceedings of the Royal Society of Medicine*

(Vol. 30) showed that great benefit was obtained by a
diet of all-raw food. At no time during the period the
diet was in operation was any salt added to the food.

We reproduce a sample day's menu:

Breakfast: Apple porridge made of grated apple,
soaked raw oatmeal, grated nuts, cream, fresh orange,
tea with milk and cream (no sugar).

Mid-morning: Tomato purée with lemon.

Dinner: Salad of lettuce, cabbage, tomato, root
vegetables, salad dressing with oil, mixed fruit salad
with cream.

Tea: Dried fruits, nuts and tea with milk and cream.

Supper: Fruit porridge, prune, apricot or apple, salad
dish with dressing.

Bedtime: Lemon and orange juice with hot water.

The dried fruits and raw oatmeal were soaked in
water, the vegetables were shredded and the nuts were
crushed or whole. All food was prepared fresh for
every meal and was served attractively.

All of the patients lost weight on the diet during the
first week, but those who continued in the following
weeks lost much less, and in every case except very
obese patients, weight was properly maintained on the
diet. For the obese patients the loss of weight was very
helpful, as overweight adds greatly to the problems of
the arthritic.

Practically all the patients showed a great
improvement after having been on the all-raw food
diet.

Avoid Salt

A diet low in salt, and preferably free from salt altogether, is most helpful in treating all forms of rheumatism. Try leaving the salt-shaker off the table and begin omitting salt from the dishes you prepare. After a time you will discover that food is more palatable when you can taste its natural flavour, instead of it being more or less heavily impregnated with salt.

Most food is adequately salted by nature. The salt we ADD is excessive. Salt often silts up the veins and arteries, stiffens the joints and makes them painful, intensifies migraine headaches, aggravates catarrh and eczema, raises blood-pressure to dangerous heights, injures the health in other ways and makes us prematurely old and decrepit.

Kelp granules sprinkled on food, will add savour and also supply essential 'trace' elements.

Sugar and Arthritis

According to a book written by Melvin Page, entitled *Degeneration – Regeneration*, an imbalance in the calcium-phosphorus ratio of the blood can bring about an arthritic condition. Dr Page found in his researches that refined white sugar, which neutralizes calcium in the blood stream is the principal factor in upsetting the normal calcium-phosphorus balance.

Refined cane sugar should be eliminated from the dietary of everyone who suffers with rheumatism and arthritis.

The Alkaline-forming Foods

The healthful alkaline-forming foods are:

Lemons	Raspberries
Oranges	Blackberries
Lettuce	Papaws
Carrots	Raisins
Tomatoes	Pineapple
Green Beans	Apples
Grapefruit	Celery
Peaches	Bananas
Grapes	Parsley
Nectarines	Peas (green)
Cherries	Apricots
Strawberries	Dried fruits
Watercress	Dates
Mint	Horseradish

In fact, fresh fruits, green vegetables and dried fruits are mostly alkaline.

Spinach and rhubarb should only be eaten in small amounts because their high oxalic acid content neutralizes some of the calcium in the blood stream. Their asset side, however, is that they are rich in iron and other minerals.

Perhaps it will be easier to remember if we put it this way: *most fruits and vegetables are alkaline-forming*.

Make a practice of having for breakfast nothing except a glass of milk and three dessertspoonsful of wheatgerm with some raisins and honey for added energy. And have a large greenleaf salad every day.

The Part Played by Vitamin A

Vitamin A acts upon the mucous membrane with which the inner surface of the body is lined. An example is the soft, pink tissue inside the mouth. Similar tissue covers the bronchial tubes, lungs, gall-bladder, urinary bladder, sinuses, inside of ears and digestive tract, as well as the tubules in the kidneys.

When the diet is lacking in vitamin A, the body becomes especially susceptible to infectious diseases. Experiments carried out on laboratory animals reveal that those deprived of vitamin A in their diet develop diseases of the lungs, kidneys, bladder, nose and throat, sinuses, mastoids, ears, etc., while animals fed adequate amounts of vitamin A, remain relatively free from such infections.

There is strong reason for belief that infections caused by lack of vitamin A, provide suitable weakened conditions in the body for rheumatism or arthritis to manifest itself.

Importance of Vitamin C

Gayelord Hauser, the famous American nutritionist, writes in *Diet Does It!*:

'Arthritis can be produced in animals by only one means – by injecting bacteria into animals whose diets lack vitamin C.

'When bacteria are injected into animals kept on exactly the same diet and given adequate vitamin C, an abscess forms at the point the bacteria are injected.

'When the abscess breaks, the bacteria are expelled from the body. Of the animals who are deficient in vitamin C, however, the bacteria can enter the blood, be carried throughout the body, and are spilled into the joints.

'Here an infection starts which, theoretically, the body tries to wall off by depositing minerals around it. Stiffness, pain and perhaps ankylosis follow.

'A number of changes occur in the body when vitamin C is under-supplied, which make it susceptible to arthritis. Half of the story in preventing arthritis is in never allowing yourself, even for one day, to be under-supplied with vitamin C.

'An abundance of vitamin C is probably more important than any other nutriment in overcoming arthritis.

'Remember that, even after the original infection is removed or cleared up, bacteria can still be carried from an already infected joint to an uninfected one, unless vitamin C is generously supplied. This vitamin is also extremely important in restoring normal cartilage.'

Rheumatism and Vitamin C Deficiency

W.J. McCormick, M.D. of Toronto, Canada, writing in the *Journal of Applied Nutrition*, considers that rheumatism and arthritis are not degenerative diseases resulting from a process of aging, but arise basically from malnutrition, and more particularly from a lack of vitamin C. He also associates rheumatism and arthritis with a form of scurvy.

Scurvy is a nutritional disorder caused by a deficiency of vitamin C. It is characterized by spongy, bleeding gums, loosening of the teeth, haemorrhages from mucous membranes, anaemia, painful hardening of the muscles, and thickening of the bones.

Dr McCormick points out that research workers found by animal experiments that a prolonged lack of vitamin C in the diet produced functional impairment and anatomical changes in the joints, typical of rheumatism and arthritis.

It is interesting to note that ailments which indicate forms of scurvy, namely, spongy gums (pyorrhea), loosening of the teeth, anaemia, painful hardening of the muscles and bone lesions, all respond to vitamin C. It is noteworthy too, that vitamin C is the most vulnerable of all vitamins. It is destroyed when vegetables become stale; it is lost by the heat of cooking, and leaches away in cooking water. Baking soda destroys it. We destroy 25 mg of vitamin C every time we smoke a cigarette. People who take aspirin and other drugs lose vitamin C rapidly.

When public surveys are conducted they reveal a general vitamin C deficiency. Thus, the US Dept. of Agriculture in a survey of 6,000 househoulds found that 25 per cent were not obtaining the bare minimum requirements of 75 mg daily, i.e., scarcely enough to prevent scurvy.

It is more than probable that a serious vitamin C deficiency also exists in Australia and that it arises from malnutrition, incorrect methods of feeding and the excessive use of tobacco and drugs. One of the results of this deficiency of vitamin C could well be the prevalence of rheumatism and arthritis and associated ailments.

Value of the Flavonoids

It is now known that vitamin C functions best when taken with the flavonoids (vitamin P). Maximum benefits are obtained (according to research workers as reported in *The Journal of American Geriatrics*) by taking these two vitamins together.

The research was conducted in America by a team of highly qualified and practical physicians. Their patients numbered 59, namely 17 with osteo-arthritis and 42 with rheumatoid arthritis. Some had suffered over a period of seven years.

The preparation used in the tests was vitamin C with hesperidin (one of the flavonoids). The dosage used was 600 mg daily of both vitamin C and hesperidin and very good results were achieved in all the cases mentioned.

Rutin, another flavonoid, gives good results with vitamin C; and hesperidin and rutin tablets are available (both with vitamin C).

The Role of B Complex Vitamins

Another important factor in building up the body's health to conquer rheumatism is to see that you have sufficient of the vitamin B complex group. There are about twelve vitamins in this group, most of them of fundamental importance to good health.

With rheumatism, the nerves and nerve sheaths in the affected part become inflamed due to being saturated with acidity. The B complex vitamins are essential to a healthy nervous system. With a sound diet and the B complex vitamins, the painful characteristics of rheumatism usually disappear gradually.

The main sources of the B complex vitamins are brewers' yeast, wheatgerm, crude molasses, wholemeal, unpolished rice, and liver. Milk and the green leaf vegetables contain a little. B complex tablets are also available.

As a general principle of good health, everybody should have three to four dessertspoonsful of wheatgerm for breakfast instead of processed cereals. Take it with plenty of milk, and some honey and raisins, which add both sweetening and energy. In addition, be sure to take one B complex vitamin tablet after each meal. Both the wheatgerm – which contains 10 of the vitamin B group – and the B complex vitamin tablets should be made a regular dietetic habit for the rest of your days.

It is also advisable to take added vitamin B_1 – one 10 mg B_1 tablet after each meal will rob arthritis of some of its pain, for this vitamin possesses analgesic as well as nutritive properties.

In his important work, *Arthritis – a Vitamin Deficiency Disease*, E.C. Barton-Wright strongly recommends pantothenic acid (calcium pantothenate) a part of the B vitamin, for osteo-arthritis, and pantothenic acid and royal jelly for rheumatoid arthritis.

Sun Baths and Vitamin D

Rheumatic and arthritic sufferers are advised by Dr Adrian Vander to take sun baths whenever possible because of their beneficial influence. Sun baths make the skin less sensitive to weather changes and improve the circulation of the blood near the skin surface. Exposure to the sun must be moderate at first to enable the skin to build up its defensive pigment, otherwise the skin may be badly burned.

The ultra-violet rays in sunlight cause the oil glands

of the skin to create a provitamin, which is converted
by the body into vitamin D and then absorbed by the
bloodstream.

During the winter months, owing to the sun's lower
altitude, and inclement weather, sunlight is weak and
intermittent and fewer ultra-violet rays reach the
earth. Vitamin D should then be taken in capsule form
to make good this deficiency. A vitamin D capsule,
taken twice daily after meals will do this, in
conjunction with one vitamin A tablet daily – not to
exceed 2,500 i.u.'s.

Vitamin D is essential for healthy bones and teeth.
It also releases energy within the body and helps to
maintain normal heart action and muscle tone.

The Merit of Vitamin E

An important corrective factor in all types of
rheumatic ailment is vitamin E.

Considerable investigation into vitamin E has been
carried out in the Arthritis Clinic, Rochester General
Hospital, Rochester, U.S.A. by Dr C.L. Steinberg.

Reporting in the *Annals of the New York Academy of
Science*, he states that he gave vitamin E to 300 patients
and relief from pain was obtained in the vast majority
of cases. He recommended that patients keep on with
a 'maintenance' dose after the symptoms have gone.
He also treated rheumatic fever successfully with
vitamin E.

Other doctors mentioned in the same journal have
reported having used vitamin E for several different
forms of rheumatism with great benefit to the patients,

i.e., relief from pain, disappearance of physical symptoms and increased mobility of joints.

Considerable success in the treatment of rheumatic heart disease by the use of vitamin E, is reported by Doctors W.E. and E.V, Shute, in their book *Alpha Tocopherol (vitamin E) in Cardiovascular Disease*.

Vitamin E improves the whole circulatory mechanism. Blood is more freely carried to the muscles and joints affected by rheumatism or arthritis. In this way the acidity in the affected parts is more readily carried away and eliminated from the system in the normal way. Conversely, the curative elements are better circulated in the affected parts.

Any factor that improves the blood supply inevitably improves the health in general and rheumatic ailments in particular.

Dr E. Tuttle, a New York physician, told a British Commonwealth Medical Congress that osteo-arthritis is not only simple wear and tear on the joints as had been long thought. It starts with a deficiency of oxygen in the cell and then goes on to destroy the cell.

Vitamin E is most beneficial in assuring the cell of adequate oxygen. It does this by decreasing the oxygen *requirement* by almost fifty per cent. This is equivalent to *increasing* the normal flow of blood by the same amount. Vitamin E not only conserves oxygen, but it strengthens muscular tissue as well. Vitamin E also increases very considerably the curative effect of vitamin A.

To obtain the maximum benefit, one vitamin E 50 mg tablet should be taken three times daily after meals.

Vitamin B$_{12}$

Vitamin B$_{12}$ (one of the B complex vitamins) has produced good results in osteo-arthritis and spondylitis, when used in conjunction with the other vitamins we advise for these diseases, as detailed later in the book under 'Vitamin Dosage'.

Vitamin B$_{12}$ is found in liver, but liver is unpalatable if eaten frequently.

Lecithin and Rheumatic Diseases

Lecithin promotes the diffusibility of blood calcium through the cell membrane, increases blood iodine and assists in the assimilation of organic phosphorus. Lecithin is also needed for the formation of healthy collagen, (which is part of the connective tissues, cartilage, and bone) according to the Lee Foundation for Nutritional Research, Milwaukee, U.S.A.

It is significant that rheumatic and arthritic ailments are most prevalent in highly civilized countries where food processing and the hydrogenation of dietary fats are customary. Such processing robs food of its lecithin content.

The Need for Iodine

D.T. Quigley, M.D., F.A.C.S., in his book, *The National Malnutrition*, says: 'Iodine, since it has to do with increasing the anti-bactericidal elements in the blood, is of value in every type of rheumatic disease.'

Iodine is contained in kelp tablets, mentioned later in this book, under 'Vitamin Dosage'.

Calcium and Arthritis

Calcium is needed by every cell in the body. Ninety-eight per cent of the body's calcium is contained in the bones and teeth, and the nerves, muscles, and various organs all depend for their health on healthy bones. Calcium is essential to muscular health and a lack of calcium can give rise to cramps and convulsions. The heart is a muscle and calcium is needed to regulate its rhythmic beat.

Is there any danger of getting too much calcium? With all the talk nowadays about calcification some people thing that ingesting too much calcium may cause arthritis. The fact is that the body is excreting calcium continuously and the danger of obtaining too much calcium is an extremely remote possibility.

The Australian dietary is very likely to be *deficient* in calcium, according to Professor Sir Stanton Hicks, eminent nutritional scientist.

Dr L.W. Cromwell of San Diego, California, reported to the Gerontological Society of San Francisco that he had found calcium *deficiency* to be a cause of arthritic crippling.

This deficiency, he said, leads first to osteoporosis (loss of bone substance). Then, owing to depletion of bone calcium, the body compensates by depositing extra calcium at the points of greatest stress – the joints – which gives rise to increased structural rigidity at the joints.

The regular consumption of calcium tablets can help to correct the osteoporotic condition mentioned and the stimulus for the body to deposit extra calcium around the bone joints, thereby causing the stiffness and swelling of arthritis.

THE SWEAT THERAPY

The human body makes use of fevers as a natural method of loosening and expelling poisonous and waste substances. A fever is thus a powerful curative agency, for by its heat it also burns up bacteria and their poisons.

A local inflammation is actually a local fever in which the affected tissue is trying to rid itself of toxic matter. By inducing sweating artificially, a rise in temperature can be produced that has similar curative properties to fever. Copious perspiration rids the body not only of the usual waste products of perspiration, i.e., water, acids, salts, etc., but also of poisonous matter which is causing sickness or retarding recovery.

For this reason, various ways of inducing perspiration have long been used successfully in rheumatic ailments. These sweating methods have the additional advantage that they also relieve pain.

We now review some of the simplest methods of inducing perspiration.

By Movement

The patient dresses in warm woollen underclothes and over it wears warm clothing and an overcoat. He now takes a long vigorous walk in the sun. After half-an-hour or so he will begin to perspire freely, and this can be kept up as long as required. At first the patient will feel oppressively hot, but once sweating starts and the poisonous matter begins to be expelled, there is a feeling of strength.

The patient should then return home, undress quickly, take a cool shower, and go to bed. This treatment should be kept up for several days in succession. In dull weather, a hot lemon drink should be taken before commencing the walk.

For those with high blood-pressure or heart ailments, the above therapy is obviously unsuitable.

Bed Sweating

If the patient for any reason is unfit to induce perspiration by walking, he should be wrapped in a dry sheet and one or two blankets (but should be able to move his arms, although they are covered). Hot water bottles should be placed at his feet and each side of him and hot lemon drinks given. The patient should begin to perspire profusely after half-an-hour or so. The period of sweating should be followed by a cool shower and then back to bed. Alternatively, the patient can be given a rub down with a towel dipped in tepid water.

The Steam Bath

A simple steam bath can be taken in the home by using a stool or kitchen chair, beneath which one or more containers of boiling water are placed. The patient sits down and a sheet and several blankets are placed around him so that the steam cannot escape, (leaving the head free). As a container of water cools another one with boiling water should be substituted. The first bath should not exceed twenty minutes and as many as two or three steam baths weekly may be taken with advantage to health.

Partial Steam Baths

These may be taken for lumbago, sciatica and rheumatism around the hips. Proceed as for an ordinary steam bath, but drape the sheet and blankets no higher than the hips, and cover the upper part of the body where no steam can reach, to keep it warm.

A partial steam bath for the head and chest is beneficial in rheumatism of the shoulder joints, between the ribs, and the chest muscles. The patient sits facing another chair back and leans the upper part of his body over a vessel of hot water. He is covered with a blanket so that no steam can escape. A cool shower should be taken after the bath, which should not last longer than from ten to fifteen minutes.

A partial steam bath can be taken for legs and feet by those with rheumatism in the lower limbs, gout, or inflammation of the knee. The container of boiling water is placed near a low stool upon which the legs are rested, and covered with a blanket to retain the steam. After the bath, the legs and feet should be washed and then rested with the legs raised.

Benefits of Steam and Other Baths

When the body is exposed to steam, the temperature of the blood rises and the heat is transmitted to inner organs. The circulation of the blood and the heart's rhythmic action are thereby stimulated and the blood-pressure rises.

Sweating should occur after a few minutes' exposure to steam, but in some instances thirty or more minutes may be needed to induce copious perspiration. An intense perspiration should be sought as this provides maximum curative benefits, not only for the skin, which as an organ of elimination contains many millions of functioning pores, but also for the kidneys, liver and lungs. Perspiration can be increased during the bath by hot lemon drinks. After the steam bath, a tepid shower should be taken and the patient should go to bed.

Because of their effect upon the blood-pressure, steam baths should not be taken by those with severe heart ailments or high blood-pressure, not should they be continued for extended periods by anyone, as they tire the heart.

Hot and Cold Baths

Hot water causes tense and stiffened muscles, joints,

and ligaments to relax. It also promotes the circulation of blood through congested areas where pain is located. Every hot bath should be followed by a cold shower. The application of cold water prevents the hot bath from having an enervating effect upon the skin. Cold water, applied in moderation to the skin, has a tonic effect, causing blood to return to the surface and speeding up the circulation. A quick rub down after the cold shower restores vitality both to the skin and the nerve endings just beneath the skin.

Water Compresses

The damp pack or water compress is applied by wringing out a bed sheet in lukewarm or cool water and spreading it over two blankets. The patient is laid on the damp sheet, which is folded around him. The two blankets should then be folded separately and neatly around the patient and a quilt placed on top. The head should be placed in a comfortable posture.

A sheet of plastic material, or even several sheets of newspaper, placed below the dampened bedsheet will prevent the mattress from becoming wet. The body, after the initial sensation of coldness, soon begins to glow. As the compress warms up, a soothing, pleasurable feeling is experienced. Pain is relieved and a profuse perspiration commences. If the patient falls off to sleep it is wise not to disturb him, but after he awakes a' tepid or cool shower should be taken to remove impurities adhering to the skin, and he should then return to bed.

The Leg Pack

This pack is useful for rheumatism or arthritis in the leg, for gout, and for varicose veins. The easiest way to apply it is to wring out thin stockings in cold water, put them on each leg and then over the top draw on thick dry woollen stockings. Both legs should be done together, not just the affected leg. This pack is very effective in absorbing poisonous substances from the legs.

Damp packs of a similar nature can be used for the ankles, knees, hands, wrists and arms, whenever there is pain or inflammation.

Hot Epsom Salts Bath

To hasten the elimination of uric acid from the system, it is important to induce its excretion through the pores. The hot Epsom salts bath will do this and can be taken twice weekly as follows:

Dissolve 1 lb of commercial Epsom salts in boiling water, and add to a hot bath, one-third full. Remain immersed in the bath for ten minutes. This bath should be taken before going to bed, and care exercised not to get chilled afterwards. Don't use soap with the Epsom salts bath, as soap interferes with its beneficial effects.

Epsom salts (magnesium sulphate) has a strong affinity for carbon and herein lies its value for medicinal purposes.

For carbon, in one form or another, is the main constituent of the building materials which go to form our vegetation and so, in turn, to provide our foodstuffs, and it is in the crude form of carbon that the waste products of the human body are thrown off.

The magnesium draws out the carbon and renders the now inert residue soluble, thereby facilitating its excretion.

Its chief value lies in its external application because of its power of drawing uric acid waste from the body through the pores of the skin.

Those who are frail and weak should begin with a small quantity, such as half a pound of Epsom salts and then gradually increase the amount as the bath becomes better tolerated. These baths are not advised for anyone with a heart condition or high blood-pressure.

The bath water should not be hotter than bloodheat, (98.6 degrees Fahr.).

TREATMENT SUMMARY

Regular bowel movement is essential. The rheumatic subject usually has a history of constipation, with the usual resort to laxative pills or medicine.

The proposed new diet should alter this condition and give you natural and regular bowel movements. The additional fruit, lettuce, celery, carrot, grated beetroot and grated apple, plus wheatgerm, molasses and the B complex vitamins, should soon get the bowels working naturally and freely.

Massage, sun bathing, exercise and dry friction skin tone up – these are all helpful and should form part of the daily practice of the rheumatic sufferer, not only during treatment, but after.

See that the kidneys function freely by drinking throughout the day glasses of diluted acid fruit juice, glasses of vegetable juice, and glasses of water. The kidneys filter uric acid from the blood and pass it out in the urine.

All the blood in the body flows through the kidneys every few minutes.

Ideal Day's Diet

The rheumatic sufferer is strongly advised to model
his diet on the following lines:

Before breakfast: A glass of diluted orange or lemon
juice (no sugar).

Breakfast: Three to four dessertspoonsful of
wheatgerm, with milk, raisins and honey. To serve the
wheatgerm with grated apple and milk is another
attractive way of taking it. Conclude breakfast with
grapes, if available, or stewed apricots, or prunes.

Mid-morning: Fruit juice, or cup of weak tea with
thin slice of bread and butter.

Lunch: Two ounces of unprocessed cheese and two
or three apples, or celery. Celery is a good source of
potassium and sodium. It is beneficial in rheumatic
ailments. No bread-stuffs.

Cheese is the one protein you require. It is a first-
class source of amino acids for tissue replacement, and
is rich in organic calcium, essential for healthy bones,
cartilage and nerves.

Afternoon: Cup of weak tea, with slice wholemeal
bread, butter and honey.

Evening meal: Large greenleaf salad, milk and fruit.
This should be preceded by a plate of hot, freshly
prepared vegetable soup in cold weather.

Before retiring: Take a dessertspoonful of molasses
which can be thinned with a little hot water, if
preferred. Molasses is rich in iron, which rheumatic
sufferers lack.

The above diet can be varied with discretion. Some
of the raw foods listed earlier can be included with
advantage. A meal of meat, fish or eggs and vegetables

is permitted two or three times per week, by way of a
change.

Vitamin Dosage

The following should be taken (all together) three
times daily before meals:—

   2 vitamin C (250 mg) tablets.
   1 vitamin E (50 mg) tablet.
   1 vitamin B-complex tablet.
   1 vitamin B_1 (10 mg) tablet.
   1 lecithin capsule (250 mg).
   1 kelp tablet (a valuable source of iodine and of
organic iron and copper, etc.).
   2 calcium tablets (white).
   1 vitamin A (2,500 i.u.) tablet should also be taken
ONCE DAILY ONLY.

NOTE: Sufferers from osteo-arthritis and
spondylitis should take two vitamin B_{12} tablets three
times daily after meals, in addition to the vitamins
listed above.

Dr Howard Hay on Arthritis

Dr Howard Hay has written in *Some Human Ailments*:

   'There is no such thing as an incurable case of arthritis,
although damage done to the joints previously by years of arthritis
may never be fully corrected. The process, however, can be halted,
and a great deal of improvement enjoyed in every case. There are
salts such as urates (any salt of uric acid) that are actually outside
the circulation, deposited in the free joint cavity, and not usually

absorbable, and so constituting a permanent crippling to just this extent.

'I would not touch starch or sugar in any form, but would live entirely on cooked vegetables, raw vegetable salads, fresh fruit and milk or butter-milk and cheese. In addition, I would suggest that you get a preparation of wheatgerm and take a tablespoonful of this three times a day with honey . . .

'It is not unusual to have a marked aggravation of the arthritis after you first begin changing the body's chemistry, and this is caused not by anything you are eating, but by chemicals already stored in your body that are still being precipitated. Go on in this way for a number of weeks, and you will find the condition arrested, for the pain is less and the attacks of acute arthritis less frequent and less severe.'

Final Word

The rheumatic sufferer, armed with the requisite knowledge set out in this book, is able to work out his own salvation from rheumatism in any of its forms. All that is required in addition to this knowledge is the will to persevere and the common sense to understand that a deep-seated arthritic condition that has taken probably fifty years to create, cannot be cured in a month. Such an expectation is unreasonable. Many months of faithful and intelligent application of the corrective principles and scientific nutrition are necessary before deep-seated conditions of arthritis begin to disappear.

We have known some of the most distorted cases to improve considerably – cases given up by the hospitals as incurable. One further thing is certain: rheumatism will seldom occur or return while you adhere to the remedial principles outlined.

It may take three months for your system to adapt itself t these corrective principles, but it will take six to twelve months before you see any substantial improvement in your arthritic condition. (Simpler forms of rheumatism usually improve in from two to six months.)

In two years, however, the most obstinate cases of rheumatoid or osteo-arthritis should show definite signs of improvement and long before this the pain should have eased and your general health be greatly improved. From that point onwards the benefits obtained are in your own hands. It is all a matter of how consistently and intelligently you apply the corrective measures day after day, month after month, and year after year.

The prospect of a long struggle to save one's life and regain one's health will deter people of weak resolution from making the effort, but those who have the *WILL* will reap life's richest reward – improved health.

Other books for better health the natural way.

LIVING WITH ANGINA
R. William Thompson

Written by an angina sufferer, this book explains how to cope with the illness and live as full a life as possible. It describes the workings of the heart and how angina is caused, and the method of treatment by diet and relaxation which has helped the author. It also shows how the angina patient can adapt his working and home conditions for maximum activity and independence, and how his family can best deal with the situation.

ARTHRITIS
Help In Your Own Hands
Helen B. MacFarlane

The story of one woman's successful fight against crippling arthritis, and how she regained full use of her limbs by a combination of diet, special exercises and massage. With notes on aids and appliances available for all arthritis sufferers.

MOLASSES AND NUTRITION
Alan Moyle, N.D., M.B.N.O.A.

Explains the nutritional significance of molasses and its value in treating many disorders, including constipation, intestinal troubles and rheumatism; with an account of sugar cane harvesting and a varied selection of molasses recipes for laxative mixtures, muesli, puddings, cakes, jellies and scones.

HERBAL TEAS
For Health and Healing
Ceres

Herbal teas, apart from being much better for you than the Indian or China teas which are so popular, make delicious drinks and can 'dispel all manner of discomforts'. The author – lifelong naturalist, broadcaster and contributor to *The Times* – describes over a hundred herbs and gives instructions for making and using the teas.

SLEEPLESSNESS

Its Prevention and Cure by Natural Methods

Cyril Scott

Most people resort to drugs when they are afflicted by sleeplessness but the majority of cases require no medicinal remedies, being caused by faulty habits of living which can be corrected by following the natural therapies provided in this book. Author includes biochemic and homoeopathic prescriptions, with notes on their individual characteristics. Every method described is utterly safe and non-toxic.

HERBAL CURES OF DUODENAL ULCER AND GALL STONES

Frank Roberts

Neither surgery nor chemicals can *cure* an ulcer; at best they only temporarily alleviate painful symptoms. But the herbal remedies given in this book offer a permanent cure. Author's simple treatments have brought relief to many thousands of sufferers. He includes details of a sure method for the elimination of gall stones within twenty-four hours.

CANCER PREVENTION

Fallacies and Some Reassuring Facts

Cyril Scott

The 'fallacies' include the belief that radium and surgery can 'cure' cancer, while the 'reassuring facts' feature homoeopathic achievements, the grape cure, and a simple preventive measure which will encourage every reader: This sane and intelligent book removes much of the dread born of many misunderstandings surrounding the subject of cancer.